Grades 6–7

Written by Sue O'Connell
Illustrated by Chris Nye

Good Apple
A Division of Frank Schaffer Publications, Inc.

Dedication

To Dan, Jerri, and Erica

Editors: Joanne Corker, Kristin Eclov, Michael Batty
Cover Design: Joanne Caroselli
Book Design: Good Neighbor Press, Inc.

Good Apple
A division of Frank Schaffer Publications, Inc.
23740 Hawthorne Boulevard
Torrance, CA 90505

GA13072

Table of Contents

Introduction

Why should students write in math class? What does math instruction have to do with writing? What is math journal writing? How do you implement math writing in your busy schedule?

Since the National Council of Teachers of Mathematics (NCTM) Standards began to influence school reform, attention has been directed to the math processes of problem solving, reasoning, communication, and connections—and to how these standards should be evident in all mathematics instruction.

In the past, traditional paper and pencil tasks have required students to fill in the answers. But students need to think, discuss, and write about their mathematics at all grade levels. In the Math—The Write Way series, students write about how they arrive at their answers, justify their mathematical thinking, and describe or define math terms and processes. They are invited to provide real-world examples of math activities and, ultimately, to reflect on their learning. Through this process of constructing answers, students gain a deeper understanding of math concepts and give you a clearer idea of what they know about mathematics.

Consider the following problem:

Which number is greater: 4×10^3 or 5×10^6? Explain your answer.

Here are some ways your students might respond:

4×10^3 because I'm sure.
Wrong answer; no explanation.

5×10^6 because it's bigger.
Correct answer, but does the student understand?

5×10^6 because 5 is more than 4.
Correct answer, but the student was comparing ones digits. Does he understand exponents?

5×10^6 is greater because $5 \times 10^6 = 5 \times 1,000,000$ and $4 \times 10^3 = 4 \times 1,000$. $5,000,000$ is much larger than $4,000$. A seven-digit number is greater than a four-digit one, so 5×10^6 must be greater than 4×10^3.
Correct answer; logical reasoning.

When you ask your students to solve a math problem, they may select the correct response without really understanding the concept. But if you ask them to *explain* the process they used to solve the problem, then they need to demonstrate understanding of the concept in order to complete the task correctly. Written responses require students to have a more thorough knowledge; they also provide insight and information in assessing each student's knowledge and mastery of math concepts and skills.

How Is This Book Organized?

This book is divided into domains based on your mathematics curriculum. These include numeration, whole numbers, rational numbers, integers, geometry, measurement, statistics/data analysis, probability, and problem solving. Each section contains a series of journal pages with writing tasks and activities that coordinate with your math instruction.

The number of activities varies with each domain, since some areas are more strongly emphasized at certain grade levels. These areas lend themselves well to student discussion and writing activities. To facilitate using these activity pages, you will find an answer key at the end of the book.

How Do I Use Journal Pages?

Students need to practice their skills in mathematical communication. These abilities become stronger when students have more opportunities to write about their thinking and to discuss what they've written.

To use the journal pages in this book most effectively, select writing activities that coordinate with the math content and concepts you are teaching in class. You may use these pages throughout the school year as part of your instruction or for assessment. Students can complete the pages in class or as home assignments. You can also pair students to give them opportunities to collaborate and hear how others are thinking. Incorporating writing activities in your math units will provide you with invaluable information to assess your students' knowledge—and help them develop essential math communication skills.

What about Reflections?

The concluding journal pages (Reflections) invite students to reflect on their math learning. Students can use these pages to think about recent lessons—commenting on their understanding of math skills and concepts, verbalizing questions or areas of confusion, and contemplating ways to apply their math skills to real-world situations. You can reuse these pages as students reflect on their learning at various times throughout the year.

By reading your students' reflections, you can gain a great deal of insight into their understanding of mathematics. You may recognize concepts that need to be re-explained, processes that appear confusing, or misunderstandings that are leading to student errors. In addition, you can gain insight into whether students feel competent, frustrated, or satisfied with their math learning. Reviewing student reflection pages can become a valuable tool for assessing your own instructional practices and allow you to modify your lessons based on student feedback.

How Do I Assess Math Writing?

Writing tasks can be scored for both content (the correctness of the response) and communication (the ability to clearly express mathematical ideas). The following rubric can be used to assess students' proficiency in both areas. Student scores can range from 0 to 4 depending on their skill in responding to writing prompts.

Scoring Rubric

4—Information is correct and complete; explanation is clear and contains adequate details

3—Information is correct and complete; explanation may lack clarity or sufficient details

2—Information is partially correct or incomplete; explanation may lack clarity or sufficient details

1—Information is incorrect; explanation is unclear

0—No attempt made

When correcting student-constructed responses, remember that students may explain what they understand in different ways, without using textbook vocabulary or phrasing. Consequently, student responses will vary for many of the activities within this book. When assessing answers, read each response to determine its correctness and use the answer key for suggestions as to what might be included in correct responses.

So go ahead . . . start using the terrific math communication activities throughout this book in your own classroom today and watch your students develop greater confidence, interest, and skill in explaining and exploring mathematics.

Name _____

Perplexing Patterns

We are surrounded by patterns. They abound in plants, animals, people, and man-made objects all around us. There are also many patterns in mathematics.

1. Write the next three numbers in this pattern. Can you describe the pattern? Have a try!

    3, 9, 27, 81, _____, _____, _____, . . .

    _____

    _____

2. Write the next three numbers in these patterns:

    a) 63, 56, 49, _____, _____, _____, . . .   c) 8, 16, 24, 32, _____, _____, _____, . . .

    b) 3, 6, 12, 24, _____, _____, _____, . . .   d) 10, 12, 15, 19, _____, _____, _____, . . .

3. Try writing the next six numbers in this pattern. Then describe the pattern.

    2, 1, 4, 3, 6, 5, _____, _____, _____, _____, _____, _____, . . .

    _____

    _____

4. Write the next three letters in these patterns. See if you can describe your work!

    a) C, F, I, L, _____, _____, _____, . . .

    _____

    _____

    b) A, B, D, G, _____, _____, _____, . . .

    _____

    _____

    _____

    _____

    _____

    _____

    _____

Reproducible

Exponent Power

Our roving reporter, A. Scoop, has been searching for that amazing superhero—Exponent Man. People everywhere are amazed at the superhero's power to increase numbers. A. Scoop has cornered you, Exponent Man's best friend, and hopes that you can share some of the superhero's secrets. Are you ready for your interview?

1. "Everyone is wondering where Exponent Man got his name. What is an exponent?"

_____

_____

2. "Just yesterday, Exponent Man changed 4^3 to 64. How did he do that?"

_____

_____

_____

3. "We've heard that Exponent Man has given you some of his powers. Can you solve the following problems just the way he might?"

a) 5^4 _____

b) 7^3 _____

c) 9^2 _____

d) 6^3 _____

e) 8^4 _____

f) 12^4 _____

g) 100^3 _____

h) 22^5 _____

4. "Normally, the numbers seem to get larger when Exponent Man uses his powers. We saw him change 6^1 to 6. Is that the correct answer? Why didn't the number get larger?"

_____

_____

_____

_____

_____

_____

_____

_____

"Thanks for sharing what you know about Exponent Man's powers! Now, back to the studio."

Prime Time

Your teacher has asked you to write an article for the class paper about your unit on prime and composite numbers. Use the questions below to help you organize your ideas.

1. What is a prime number? What is a composite?

   _____
   _____
   _____

2. Think about the numbers 1–25. Which numbers are both prime and odd? Justify your answer.

   _____
   _____
   _____

3. There is only one even prime number. What is it? Why is it the only even prime number?

   _____
   _____
   _____

4. Explain how to find the prime factorization of 45.

   _____
   _____
   _____

5. Find the prime factorization of the following numbers:

   a) 24 _____   d) 300 _____

   b) 15 _____   e) 76 _____

   c) 112 _____   f) 150 _____

Name _____

What Are LCMs?

Your friend was absent when the class learned about least common multiples (LCMs). Help your friend understand LCMs by answering these questions.

1. What is a least common multiple (LCM)?

   _____

   _____

   _____

2. How do you find the least common multiple of two numbers?

   _____

   _____

   _____

3. What is the LCM of these numbers?

   a) 4, 9   _____

   b) 3, 13 _____

   c) 2, 7   _____

   d) 10, 16 _____

   e) 20, 25 _____

   f) 397, 1 _____

4. Could there be a greatest common multiple for two numbers? Why or why not?

   _____

   _____

   _____

   _____

   _____

   _____

   _____

A Number Challenge

Do you like number challenges? See how you do with this one

1. How many different numbers can you make by using the digits *6, 7,* and *8?* The numbers may have one, two, or three digits, but you may only use *6, 7,* and *8* once in each number. (This means that 777 is not a possibility, as it uses *7* more than once.) Use the space below to work out your answer.

2. Now list the numbers you made from smallest to largest.

   _____

   _____

   _____

3. Are you sure that you found all possible numbers? Justify your answer.

   _____

   _____

   _____

   _____

   _____

Reproducible

The Hidden Square

Here's a number puzzle that's all about squares. You will need to solve the problems below, squaring some numbers and finding the square roots of others. As you solve each problem, shade in your answer on the grid. If you've answered each question correctly, the grid should reveal the square root of 16.

1. Square the following numbers. Remember to shade in the answers on the grid.

   a) 5 _____   b) 10 _____   c) 13 _____   d) 15 _____   e) 25 _____

2. Find the square roots of the following numbers. Shade in the answers on the grid.

   a) 49 _____   b) 81 _____   c) 121 _____   d) 256 _____   e) 400 _____

62	10	73	15	27	713	4	57
306	0	218	42	99	421	43	519
29	89	437	75	130	920	2	14
82	18	100	60	108	25	701	95
535	126	7	19	416	20	76	500
107	639	169	11	16	225	93	164
501	1	397	900	41	9	274	450
47	15	49	480	5	625	17	12
920	82	724	13	21	342	31	627
3	74	160	6	111	821	943	8

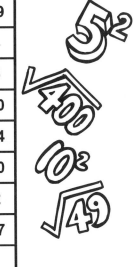

3. What is the square root of 16? Explain how you know that the answer on the grid is correct.

   _____

   _____

4. What does it mean to square a number?

   _____

   _____

Reproducible

Why Estimate?

In mathematics, we often need to calculate exact numbers. When we are at the grocery store paying for our purchases, the cashier expects to be paid the exact amount. When cutting carpet to cover an area of floor, the installer needs to know exact measurements. But there are other times when we only need to give an estimate.

1. Explain how estimation can help you in everyday life.

_____
_____
_____
_____
_____
_____
_____
_____
_____
_____

2. Describe a time when you used estimation.

_____
_____
_____
_____
_____
_____
_____
_____
_____

Tell Me a Story

Do you like telling stories? What about math stories? Write an equation for each of these situations. Then solve each equation.

1. Katie baked *c* cakes. Lisa baked 5 cakes. They baked 8 cakes altogether. Solve for *c*.

_____

2. Brendan ran *m* miles every day for five days. He ran a total of 25 miles. Solve for *m*.

_____

3. Marta had 24 pieces of fruit. She sorted them into *b* bags. Each bag had 4 pieces of fruit in it. Solve for *b*.

_____

4. Now try writing your own word problem for $6x = 30$. Solve your problem.

_____

_____

_____

5. Write a word problem for $13 + d = 22$. Solve your problem.

_____

_____

_____

6. Explain two different strategies to solve for *d*.

_____

_____

_____

Name _____

Make It Simpler

Here are some everyday math situations. Write an equation for each problem and then use inverse operations to solve your work.

1. Rosa brought $27 to the grocery store. She had $9 left when she got home. Write an addition equation to figure out how much she spent. Let *s* equal the amount spent. Use inverse operations to solve your equation.

   _____

   _____

2. Lee scored 15 points in the first half of the basketball game. He scored 32 points altogether. Write an addition equation to figure out how many points he scored in the second half. Let *p* equal the points scored in the second half. Use inverse operations to solve your equation.

   _____

   _____

3. There are 10 bags of candy with the same amount in each bag. There are 120 pieces of candy altogether. Write a multiplication equation to figure out how many pieces of candy are in each bag. Let *x* equal the pieces in each bag. Use inverse operations to solve your equation.

   _____

   _____

4. If *x* people are riding in cars and each car has six people in it, how many cars are there? Can you solve this problem? Explain why or why not.

   _____

   _____

5. Suppose you have a classmate who does not understand how to create equations from problems. Write the steps for creating an equation to solve a word problem. You may use one of the problems above as an example.

   _____

   _____

   _____

   _____

   _____

16

My Dear Aunt Sally

When simplifying an expression, it's important to know the order of operations. Some people use silly sayings to help them remember this rule. One old favorite is *My Dear Aunt Sally*—multiplication, division, addition, and subtraction. Do you know any other sayings to help remember the order operations?

1. Can you explain the order of operations rule?

   _____

   _____

   _____

   _____

   _____

2. Simplify the expression 10 + 3 x 5 and then describe the order in which you did it.

   _____

   _____

   _____

3. Simplify the expression 21 x (4 + 6) and then describe the order in which you did it.

   _____

   _____

   _____

4. Write what you would do to simplify each expression and then simplify it.

   a) 7×2^4 _____

   b) 6 x (4 + 6) _____

   c) $5^3 \times 4$ _____

   d) 26 − 16 ÷ 4 _____

   e) 4 x (8 − 5) _____

   f) 12 + 6 x 4 _____

Name _____

Predicting fractions

Do you like making predictions? See if you can correctly predict the fractions to complete these number sequences.

1. Look at this pattern and write the next three fractions: 1, $\frac{1}{2}$, $\frac{1}{3}$, $\frac{1}{4}$, ___, ___, ___, $\cdots$
   Describe the pattern.

   _____

   _____

2. Now write the next three fractions in these patterns and describe them.

   a) $\frac{1}{2}$, $\frac{1}{4}$, $\frac{1}{8}$, $\frac{1}{16}$, ___, ___, ___, $\cdots$

   _____

   _____

   b) $\frac{1}{2}$, $\frac{1}{6}$, $\frac{1}{18}$, $\frac{1}{54}$, ___, ___, ___, $\cdots$

   _____

   _____

3. Now create your own fraction pattern and then describe it.

   _____

   _____

   _____

   _____

Reproducible

© Good Apple GA13072

Making the Grade

Tests, percents, and grades are a very important part of school life. Are you making the grade?

1. On the math test, you got 17 out of 20 questions right. What was your percent correct on the test? Explain how you know.

   _____

   _____

   _____

   _____

   _____

2. 25 students took the test, and 16 students earned an A. What percentage of the students got an A? Explain how you found your answer.

   _____

   _____

   _____

3. Your teacher has informed you that you need a grade of at least 70% to pass her tests. Look at the information below and determine your scores. Explain whether you passed or failed each test.

   a) You correctly answered 75 out of 150 problems.

      Your score: _____   Pass, or fail?

   b) You correctly answered 56 out of 80 problems.

      Your score: _____   Pass, or fail?

   c) You incorrectly answered 5 out of 25 problems.

      Your score: _____   Pass, or fail?

   d) You incorrectly answered 3 out of 13 problems.

      Your score: _____   Pass, or fail?

Name _____

An Appetizing Order

Catalogs offer customers all sorts of interesting products—just like these delicious items!

Fruit Pack (A healthy selection of seasonal fruits) $23.50
Candy Mix (A variety of mouth-watering chocolates and caramels) $13.70
Nuts Galore (A tasty mix of cashews, pecans, and almonds) $17.55
Cheese and Sausage (A flavorful selection of cheeses and sausages) $28.40

1. The company charges 9% shipping and handling for each item. How much will it cost to ship a box of Candy Mix? (Round to the nearest cent.) Explain your answer.

   _____

   _____

2. You have $100 to spend on gifts from the catalog. Decide on what you will order and write your choices on this form.

Belair Farms Fine Foods
P.O. Box 90210
Belair, Maryland 21014

Items	Quantity	Price Each	Subtotal
		Subtotal	
		Shipping Cost	
		Total	

3. You want to buy as many items as possible with your $100. Which item could you buy the most of? How many could you buy? Don't forget to include shipping and handling. Explain your answer.

   _____

   _____

Reproducible

Name _____

What's the Difference?

Sometimes a small change in the spelling of a word can change its meaning—even in the world of mathematics.

1. Explain the difference between 5 tens and 5 tenths. You may use diagrams to help clarify your explanation.

_____

_____

_____

_____

_____

2. Now explain the difference between 12 hundreds and 12 hundredths. You may use diagrams again to help clarify your explanation.

_____

_____

_____

_____

_____

_____

Name _____

What's the Connection?

Your best friend is feeling very confused about decimals, fractions, and percents. Can you help answer your friend's questions?

1. "I'm looking at the number shown on this grid. How do I write this number as a decimal, fraction, and percent?"

    a) Decimal _____

    b) Fraction _____

    c) Percent _____

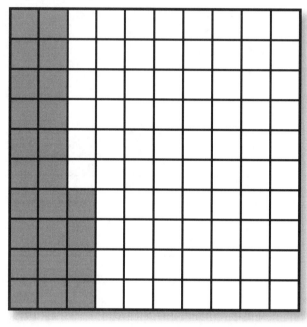

2. "How are fractions and decimals alike? How are they different?"

_____

_____

_____

_____

_____

_____

3. "And what about decimals and percents? How are they alike? How are they different?"

_____

_____

_____

_____

_____

22

Reproducible

Name _____

The Parking Lot Predicament

The school parking lot is about to be repaved. The principal asks you to go outside and see how many vehicles must be moved from the lot. You see 30 vehicles on the lot—3 motorcycles, 6 trucks, 15 cars, and 6 bicycles. So you go inside and give your report to the principal.

1. Your principal asks you to use fractions to describe the number of vehicles that are cars, motorcycles, trucks, and bicycles. (Remember to reduce each fraction to its lowest terms.)

_____

2. The vice principal enters, and you tell him that there are 30 vehicles in the lot today. He asks you to use decimals to tell him about the vehicles.

_____

3. Now you return to your classroom and tell your teacher that there are 30 vehicles in the parking lot. Big mistake! Your teacher asks you to use percents to tell her more about the vehicles.

_____

4. Finally, you decide to create a circle graph to show everyone the types of vehicles in the parking lot today. Draw and label your graph below.

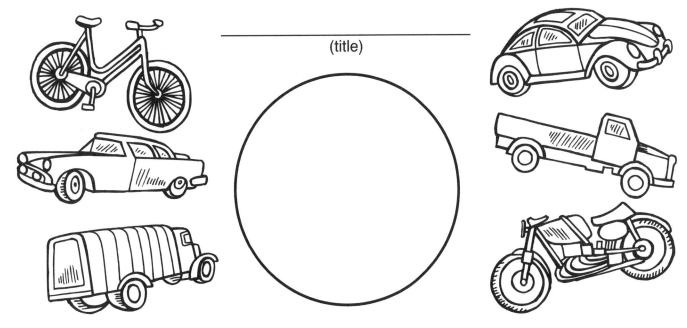

_____
(title)

5. Was it easy or hard to create a circle graph for this data? Why or why not? How might this graph help you? Write your answer on the back of this page.

Name _____

Can You Help?

Your best friend has just whispered, "Can you help me?" Your friend is having trouble adding and subtracting fractions with different denominators. Can you help your friend?

Solve each problem below and then explain the steps you followed to solve the problem.

1. $\dfrac{6}{7} - \dfrac{1}{4} =$ _____

_____

_____

_____

_____

_____

_____

2. $\dfrac{2}{5} + \dfrac{1}{3} =$ _____

_____

_____

_____

_____

_____

_____

24

Name _____

Palatable Portions

Is Deep Chocolate Cake your favorite? Wouldn't it be great if you could bake one slice whenever you wanted a snack?

Deep Chocolate Cake

$\frac{1}{3}$ cup butter

$1\frac{3}{4}$ cups sugar

2 cups flour

$\frac{1}{2}$ cup cocoa

2 teaspoons baking powder

$\frac{1}{2}$ teaspoon baking soda

3 eggs

$1\frac{1}{2}$ cups milk

1 teaspoon vanilla

---

1. This recipe makes eight delicious servings. But how much of each of the following ingredients is in one serving? (Use fractions.)

   a) Butter _____   d) Cocoa _____   g) Eggs _____

   b) Sugar _____   e) Baking powder _____   h) Milk _____

   c) Flour _____   f) Baking soda _____   i) Vanilla _____

2. Explain how you determined the amount of ingredients in one serving.

   _____

   _____

3. Would it be difficult to bake just one serving of cake? Why or why not?

   _____

   _____

4. A serving of cake is $\frac{1}{8}$ of a cake. If you have $1\frac{3}{4}$ cakes, how many servings do you have? Explain your answer.

   _____

   _____

Name _____

On the Ratio Trail

Knowing all about ratios helps with many everyday activities, including cooking dinner, drawing pictures, building houses, and designing clothes.

1. What is a ratio? Explain your answer and then write three ratios below.

    _____

    _____

    _____

2. Examine this recipe for Trail Mix. What is the ratio of raisins to peanuts? _____

Trail Mix

24 raisins

16 peanuts

30 pretzels

32 miniature marshmallows

3. Let's look for some more ratios in this recipe.

    a) What is the ratio of marshmallows to pretzels? _____

    b) What is the ratio of peanuts to marshmallows? _____

    c) What is the ratio of raisins to pretzels? _____

4. Write another ratio for this Trail Mix.

    _____

    _____

    _____

Name _____

Proportional Puzzlers

Now that you know all about ratios, it's time to explore proportions. And like ratios, proportions are all around us!

1. Look at these two ratios: $\frac{2}{3} = \frac{4}{9}$. Are these ratios proportional? Why or why not?

_____

_____

2. So, what is a proportion?

_____

_____

3. Write a proportion for each of the following fractions:

a) $\frac{2}{5} =$ _____

b) $\frac{1}{4} =$ _____

c) $\frac{3}{4} =$ _____

d) $\frac{7}{9} =$ _____

e) $\frac{2}{3} =$ _____

f) $\frac{1}{2} =$ _____

4. Imagine that there is one table for every five chairs in a Mexican fast-food restaurant. Write a proportion to show the number of chairs for six tables.

_____

5. If you get paid $6 per hour, write a proportion to show how much you get paid for six hours.

_____

6. How do you solve a proportion that has a variable? Explain the process by using the problem $\frac{2}{5} = \frac{x}{40}$.

_____

_____

_____

_____

_____

_____

Name _____

Delicious Deals

Understanding mathematics can help you find some delicious deals at the grocery store!

Toasty Oats $1.65/14.5 oz. box
Corn Munchies $2.30/16 oz. box
Checkers $1.85/15 oz. box

1. Which cereal is the best buy? Compute the unit price to determine the best buy. Justify your answer with math data.

_____
_____
_____
_____

2. Steak is on sale this week for $3.88 per pound. It usually costs $5.99 per pound. The meat you are buying weighs 2.5 pounds. How much will it cost? Explain how you figured out the cost.

_____
_____
_____

3. How much did you save by buying steak this week? Explain your answer.

_____
_____
_____

4. Think about this: Does a five-pound bag of potatoes indicate an exact weight of five pounds or an estimate? Explain your answer.

_____
_____
_____

Name _____

A Super Sale

Everyone loves a bargain. Let's explore this super sale!

1. The video game you've been wanting is on sale this week. The original price was $35.00, but the game is on sale for 20% off. How much will the game cost this week? Explain how you figured out your answer.

_____

_____

2. The video store has a Super Saturday Sale. On Super Saturday, customers receive an additional 10% off the sale price. How much will the video game cost on Super Saturday? Explain how you determined this special price.

_____

_____

3. Complete the table below to show the sale price and Super Saturday price for each item.

Items	Original price	Sale price 20% off	Super Saturday price Additional 10% off sale price
Video games	$ 35.00		
CDs	$ 20.00		
CD storage case	$ 13.00		
Cassette tapes	$ 9.50		
Video play station	$140.00		

4. If you buy one of each item during the Super Saturday Sale, what will be your total savings compared to the original cost? Explain how you determined your total savings.

_____

_____

Name _____

Batter Up!

Bankers aren't the only people who like decimals! These numbers abound in the world or sports!

1. Here are the batting averages of ten players. Put the players in order from worst batting average to best.

Steven	.310	1. _____
Rodney	.331	2. _____
Michael	.278	3. _____
Kevin	.253	4. _____
Joe	.257	5. _____
Andrew	.279	6. _____
Chris	.290	7. _____
Ryan	.215	8. _____
Patrick	.275	9. _____
Jason	.301	10. _____

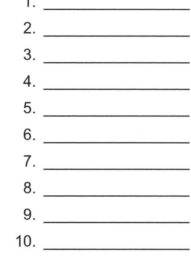

2. Explain how you put decimals in order.

_____

_____

_____

3. List some examples of ways that decimals are used in the real world.

_____

_____

_____

_____

_____

_____

Reproducible

Name _____

Inquiring about Integers

Your cousin is having a hard time understanding integers. Answer your cousin's questions to help him or her become an integer expert.

1. "What is an integer?"

   _____

   _____

   _____

2. "Is 3.5 an integer? Why or why not?"

   _____

   _____

3. "How do you solve this problem: 4 + -6 = ?"

   _____

   _____

   _____

4. "How can I add integers with a number line?" (Show an example on the number line below.)

   _____

   _____

   _____

   _____

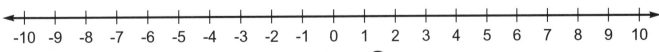

Reproducible   **31**

Name _____

Positive or Negative?

Your teacher has asked you to prepare a report for your class on adding and subtracting integers. Use the questions below to help you prepare your thoughts for the report.

1. When you add two negative integers, is the sum positive or negative? Explain your answer.

   _____
   _____
   _____
   _____
   _____
   _____
   _____

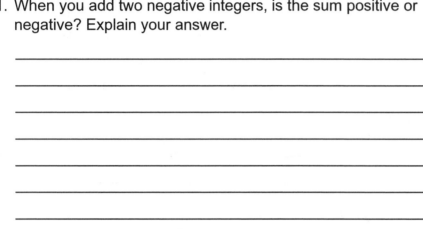

2. Does -9 + 2 equal 2 + (-9)? Justify your answer.

   _____
   _____
   _____
   _____
   _____

3. When you subtract a negative number, is the result greater than or less than the original number? Why or why not?

   _____
   _____
   _____
   _____

Reproducible

Name _____

Absolutely Positive!

Your grandma is interested in what you've learned about absolute value. Use the questions below to tell her what you know.

1. What is absolute value?

_____

_____

2. Use this number line to help explain absolute value.

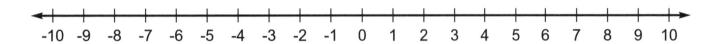

-10 -9 -8 -7 -6 -5 -4 -3 -2 -1 0 1 2 3 4 5 6 7 8 9 10

3. What is the absolute value of a positive number? Justify your answer.

_____

_____

_____

4. What is the absolute value of a negative number? Justify your answer.

_____

_____

_____

5. Solve:

a) $|3|$ = _____   c) $|0|$ = _____   e) $|-3.5|$ = _____

b) $|-10|$ = _____   d) $|6.34|$ = _____   f) $|\frac{1}{2}|$ = _____

Name _____

Check It Out!

Your parents have just opened a checking account for you. They deposited $100 in the account to get you started.

1. On your first shopping spree, you bought a shirt and wrote a check to Express Clothing for $32.00. You also bought a CD and wrote a check to CD World for $12.00. Then you cut the neighbor's grass and earned $23.00, which you deposited into your account. Finally, you wrote a check to Ticket Max for $27.00 worth of concert tickets. How much money is in your account now? Explain how you determined this answer.

_____

_____

_____

_____

2. Complete the checkbook below to show what has been happening with your account.

Transaction Description	Amount of Payment or Withdrawal	Amount of Deposit	Balance
Deposit		$100.00	$100.00

Reproducible

© Good Apple GA13072

Name _____

Meet Mr. or Ms. Write Angle

Imagine that you are Mr. or Ms. Write Angle, the best math teacher in the school!

1. Prepare a lesson for your class. Your students need to understand how to find the measure of Angle *ABC*. Be sure to describe the tool they should use and how to place it on the page so that they get the correct measurement. And don't forget to tell your students how to decide which number on the tool indicates the correct angle measurement.

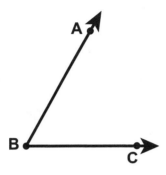

_____

_____

_____

_____

_____

2. What is the measure of ∠*ABC*? _____

3. Some of your students are confused about acute, obtuse, and right angles. They can't decide which angle is which! Give your students some tips to help them understand these angles.

_____

_____

_____

4. Now draw and label these three angles (acute, obtuse, and right) for your students.

Name _____

What's the Angle?

It's time to test your knowledge about angles.

1. What are complementary angles?

   _____
   _____

2. What are supplementary angles?

   _____
   _____

3. If two angles combine to form a complementary angle, can both of the original angles be obtuse angles? Justify your answer.

   _____
   _____
   _____
   _____
   _____
   _____

4. If two angles combine to form a supplementary angle, and one of the angles is a right angle, what is the measure of the other angle? Explain your answer.

   _____
   _____
   _____
   _____

5. If two angles combine to form a complementary angle, can either of the original angles be obtuse? Justify your answer.

   _____
   _____
   _____
   _____

Name _____

Do You Know Your Shapes?

How about exploring some special shapes? How well do you know them?

1. Draw and label a rhombus, a parallelogram, and a trapezoid.

2. Now define a rhombus, a parallelogram, and a trapezoid.

_____

_____

_____

3. Write true or false for each statement below; then justify your answer.

a) All parallelograms are quadrilaterals. _____

_____

_____

b) A rhombus is not a parallelogram. _____

_____

_____

c) A trapezoid is a rhombus. _____

_____

_____

What Shape Is That Number?

Some numbers are described as triangular numbers, and others as square ones. Let's explore some numbers to find out what gives them their shapes!

Triangular numbers can be represented by dots that are arranged in triangles.

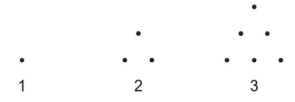

1   2   3

1. How many dots will be in the 6th triangle? _____

2. How many dots will be in the 12th triangle? _____

3. How might you figure this out without drawing all of the triangles?

_____

_____

_____

Square numbers can be represented by dots that are arranged in squares.

1   2   3

4. How many dots will be in the 6th square? _____

5. How many dots will be in the 12th square? _____

6. How might you figure this out without drawing all of the squares?

_____

_____

_____

Name _____

Metric Choices

Choosing the correct unit of measure is very important. If you were asked to measure the distance from the school office to your classroom, would you measure it in millimeters? Centimeters? Meters? Kilometers? Choosing the best unit of measure will make your job easier. Think about the situations below and choose the unit of measure to simplify each job.

1. If you were to measure the perimeter of your desktop, which metric unit would you use? Why?

   _____

   _____

2. If you were to measure the distance from one city to another, which metric unit would you use? Why?

   _____

   _____

3. If you were to measure the length of a paper clip, which metric unit would you use? Why?

   _____

   _____

4. Make a list of items that you might measure by using the following:

Millimeters	Centimeters	Meters

Name _____

Going in Circles

Let's explore circles! Come on, we're on a roll!

1. How is the perimeter (*P*) of a rectangle like the circumference (*C*) of a circle? How are they different?

   _____

   _____

   _____

2. Explain the symbol π (pi).

   _____

   _____

3. How do you determine the circumference of a circle? Explain your answer.

   _____

   _____

4. What is the circumference of each circle below?

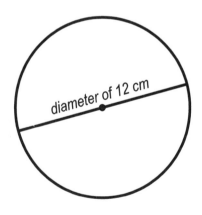
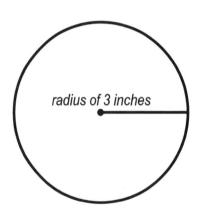
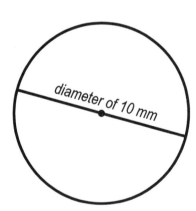

diameter of 12 cm   radius of 3 inches   diameter of 10 mm

a) *C* = _____   b) *C* = _____   c) *C* = _____

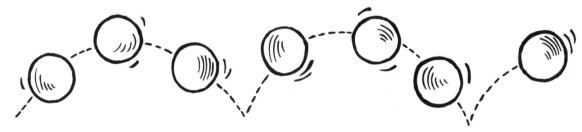

Reproducible

Name _____

Calculating Cookies

Your friend loves chocolate chip cookies, so you decide to buy a giant birthday cookie for your friend's surprise party. But you want to get the best delicious deal!

1. The Cookie Place makes cookies of all shapes and sizes. Here are the prices for two giant birthday cookies. Use the information below to decide which cookie is the best buy. Justify your answer with mathematical data.

   10" x 14" cookie—$6.50   10" round cookie—$4.50

   _____

   _____

   _____

   _____

2. Using the example of a giant cookie with a 12 inch diameter, explain how to compute the area (*A*) of a circular region. Draw and label a diagram to go along with your explanation.

   _____

   _____

   _____

   _____

   _____

3. Using the example of an 8.5" x 11" birthday brownie, explain how to compute the area of rectangular regions. Draw and label a diagram to go along with your explanation.

   _____

   _____

   _____

   _____

   _____

Name _____

Puzzling Parallelograms

You will recall that a parallelogram is a four-sided figure with opposite sides that are parallel and the same length. Let's puzzle over some parallelograms!

1. Label the height (3 cm) and base (5 cm) of the parallelogram below. Draw a dotted line to show where the height is measured.

2. How do you find the area of a parallelogram? What is the area of the parallelogram above?

_____

_____

_____

_____

3. Find the area of parallelograms with the following measurements:

   a) b = 6 mm, h = 12 mm _____

   b) b = 13 m, h = 21 m _____

   c) b = 17 cm, h = 19 cm _____

   d) b = 2.9 m, h = 3.6 m _____

   e) b = 495 km, h = 1,210 km _____

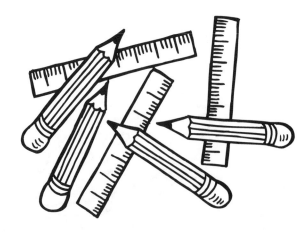

Name _____

Getting Ready for the Big Test

You have been asked to create a study sheet for your class. This guide will help your friends find the areas of rectangles, squares, parallelograms, triangles, and circles.

To make your study sheet, draw each geometric figure and write the formula for figuring out its area. Label your drawings and include any tips to help your friends remember the formulas.

Study Tips

_____

_____

_____

_____

_____

_____

_____

Measurement

Sport Sketches

Architects make scale drawings when they plan buildings. Engineers use them when they build roads and parks. A scale drawing is a sketch that is similar to the actual area. The ratios of actual measurements and of measurements for the scale drawing should be equivalent.

1. Here's your chance! Create a scale drawing of a football field that is 100 yards long and 50 yards wide. (Use a copy of the grid on page 45 for your drawing.)

2. What scale did you use for your sketch? Why?

   _____

   _____

   _____

3. a) What is the area of the actual field? _____ b) What is the perimeter? _____

4. A tennis court is 78 feet long and 36 feet wide. Create a scale drawing of the court on the grid. (Use a copy of the grid on page 45 for your drawing.)

5. What scale did you use for your sketch? Why?

   _____

   _____

   _____

6. a) What is the area of the actual court? _____ b) What is the perimeter? _____

Challenge: Research the dimensions of other sports playing fields and create scale drawings.

Reproducible

© Good Apple GA13072

Name ____

Measurement

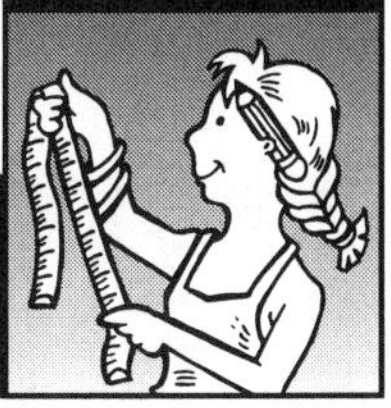

A Field of Play

____
(title)

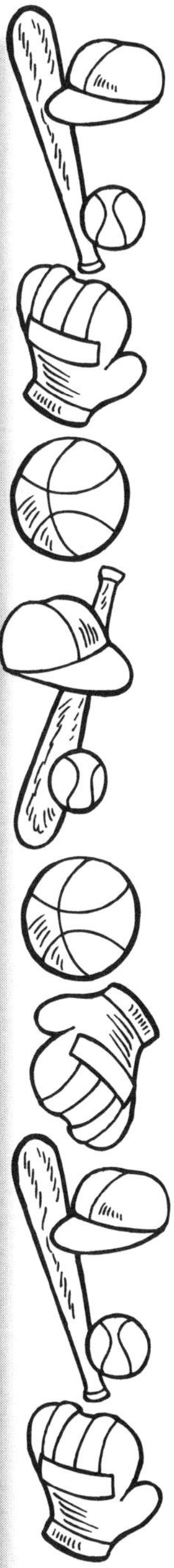

Name _____

Metric Fun and Games

Create a game to help your friends understand metric measures of length. Explain your game below—including the rules and how winners are determined. Remember that the object of your game is to help students understand the following metric measures of length:

1,000 millimeters (mm) = 1 meter (m)
100 centimeters (cm) = 1 meter (m)
10 decimeters (dm) = 1 meter (m)
1,000 meters (m) = 1 kilometer (km)

_____
_____
_____
_____
_____
_____
_____
_____
_____
_____
_____
_____
_____
_____
_____

_____
_____
_____
_____
_____
_____
_____
_____
_____

A Matter of Age

Most of your classmates are probably about the same age. But what about your teachers?

Ages of Teachers at Yorktown School
22, 24, 49, 43, 47, 24, 32, 35, 22, 24, 28, 29, 24, 26, 21, 41, 28, 60, 44, 41

1. Use this data to create a stem and leaf plot.

Stems	Leaves

2. What is the range of teachers' ages at the school? Explain how to find the range.

_____

_____

3. What is the mode? Explain how to find the mode.

_____

_____

4. What is the median? Explain how to find the median.

_____

_____

5. What is the mean age of teachers at Yorktown? Explain how to find the mean. Why is the mean of this data greater than the median?

_____

_____

6. What conclusions can you draw from this data?

_____

_____

Name _____

Which Would You Choose?

Here's a wide variety of facts and figures. Take a careful look at the information; then say which type of graph you would choose to represent each piece of data. Be sure to justify your choice.

1. Costs of college education from 1960–2000

   _____

   _____

   _____

   _____

2. Favorite travel destinations for members of our class

   _____

   _____

   _____

   _____

3. Ages of U.S. presidents when inaugurated

   _____

   _____

   _____

   _____

4. Favorite board games of second graders and sixth graders

   _____

   _____

   _____

   _____

5. The number of hot dogs sold each month during baseball season at a major league baseball stadium

   _____

   _____

   _____

   _____

Reproducible

Name _____

Michael's Awesome Achievements

Do you have a sports hero? Perhaps one of your favorites is Michael Jordan. He certainly has some awesome achievements!

1. Complete the following table showing Michael Jordan's career statistics.

Season	Games Played	Total Points	Average Points per Game (to nearest tenth)	Scoring Rank (#1 is best)
1984–85	82	2,313	28.2	
1985–86	18	408	22.7	
1986–87	82	3,041		
1987–88	82	2,868	35.0	
1988–89		2,633	32.5	
1989–90	82	2,753		
1990–91	82	2,580	31.5	
1991–92	80	2,404		
1992–93	78	2,541	32.6	
1993–94	Did not play this year.			
1994–95	17		26.9	
1995–96	82	2,491		
1996–97	82	2,431	29.6	
1997–98	82	2,357	28.7	
Career totals	930	29,277		XXXX

2. Explain how to calculate Michael's average points per game for a season.

_____

3. Use the data about Michael's average points scored per game to rank his seasons from best-scoring to worst. Record the ranks in the last column of the table. What math skill do you need to know in order to rank the seasons?

_____

4. What were Michael's average points scored per game for his total career? In which seasons did Michael average more points per game than his career scoring average? Explain how you know.

_____

_____

Name _____

Picturing Michael's Accomplishments

1. Create a graph to show Michael's average points scored per game for each season of his career. Write a title for your graph and label the x and y axes.

_____
(title)

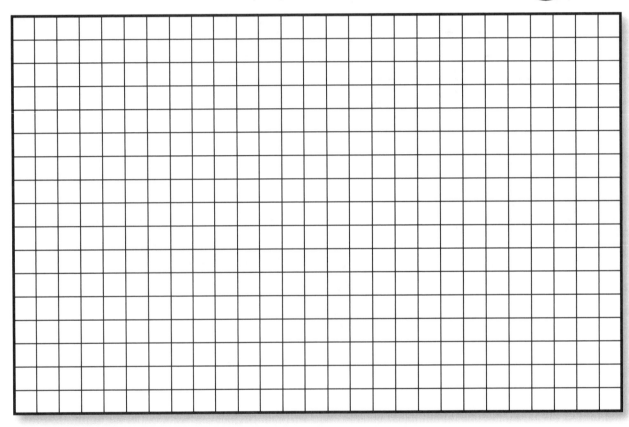

2. What type of graph did you choose? Why?

_____

_____

3. What does the graph show? What are your observations and conclusions?

_____

_____

_____

Reproducible

The Name Game

Mrs. Alexander's class is investigating the number of letters in people's first names. Here is a list of the students in her class.

Mrs. Alexander's Students

Susan	Catherine	John	Marie
Chi	Roberto	Kim	Mario
Martin	Michael	Christy	David
Ed	Gerri	Clarice	Ling

1. Create a line plot to show the number of letters in each person's first name. Be sure to include a title for your work.

_____
(title)

| 1 | 2 | 3 | 4 | 5 | 6 | 7 | 8 | 9 | 10 |

2. Find the range, median, mean, and mode of the data, each rounded to the nearest tenth.

a) Range _____   b) Median _____   c) Mean _____   d) Mode _____

3. Is a line plot a good choice for displaying this data? Why or why not?

_____

4. Would you classify your name as short, long, or average? Use math to justify your answer.

_____

_____

Name _____

Got the Munchies?

Students at Rockledge School love to buy candy from the school vending machine. The data below shows how much candy Rockledge students bought in a single day.

1. Create a graph to represent the data. Write a title for your graph and label the *x* and *y* axes.

Time	# Sold
7:00 a.m.	1
8:00 a.m.	5
9:00 a.m.	7
10:00 a.m.	10
11:00 a.m.	23
12:00 noon	35
1:00 p.m.	28
2:00 p.m.	17
3:00 p.m.	39
4:00 p.m.	48
5:00 p.m.	23
6:00 p.m.	19
7:00 p.m.	35
8:00 p.m.	40

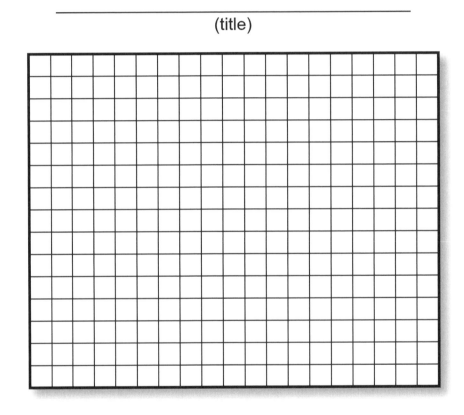

_____
(title)

2. Which increments did you choose for displaying the candy data? Why?

_____

3. Explain the data. Why might it look the way it does?

_____

_____

4. Who might be interested in this data? Why?

_____

_____

Statistics/Data Analysis

Top It Off! (1)

What do you like on your pizza? Do adults and children like the same kinds of toppings? Let's find out!

1. For homework, survey ten people to determine their favorite pizza topping. Here are the rules:

   a) Question five people who are under 18 years old. (No class members allowed.)

   c) Question five people who are 18 years old or older.

   d) Topping choices are pepperoni, sausage, mushroom, green pepper, onion, and anchovy.

2. Record your homework survey results below.

Favorite Topping						
	Pepperoni	Sausage	Mushroom	Green pepper	Onion	Anchovy
People under 18						
People 18 and over						

3. When you return to class, you will be combining your results with the findings of other students. Predict what your group data may show.

_____

_____

_____

_____

_____

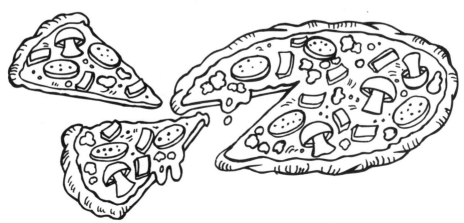

Name _____

Top It Off! (2)

Now it's time to organize and represent your pizza topping findings.

1. Working with a group of four to six students, combine your homework survey results on this table.

Favorite Topping						
	Pepperoni	**Sausage**	**Mushroom**	**Green pepper**	**Onion**	**Anchovy**
People under 18						
People 18 and over						

2. Design a double bar graph to show the results of your survey. Write a title for your graph and label the *x* and *y* axes.

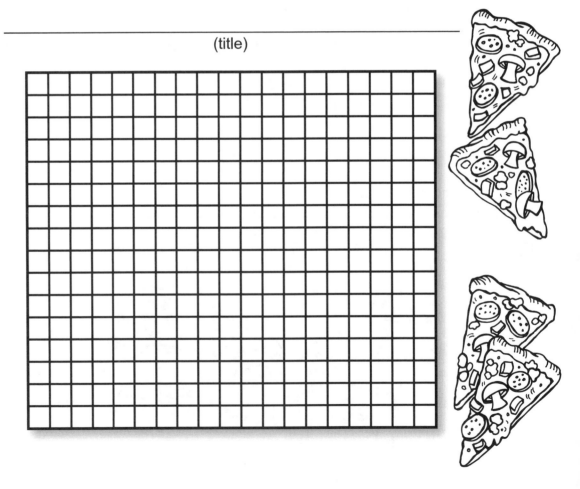

_____
(title)

Reproducible

© Good Apple GA13072

Name _____

Top It Off! (3)

Finally, it's time to describe and interpret your data.

1. Examine the data on your graph and describe the results. Be sure to include the most popular toppings for adults and children. Use fractions or percents to describe some of the data.

_____

_____

_____

_____

2. Present your graph to the class. How does your graph compare with those created by other groups? Explain your answer.

_____

_____

_____

3. Did any of the results surprise you? Why or why not? Did they match your predictions?

_____

_____

_____

4. If you were ordering five pizzas for a second-grade party, which toppings would you order? What if you were ordering five pizzas for a teachers' luncheon? Justify your orders by using the data you collected.

_____

_____

_____

_____

_____

_____

_____

_____

Name _____

Watching It Grow

Your class is doing a science investigation on the growth of plants. You have measured the height of your plant each week for the past seven weeks. Here is the data you collected:

Week 1: 2 cm   Week 5: 4.7 cm
Week 2: 3 cm   Week 6: 4.8 cm
Week 3: 3.6 cm   Week 7: 4.8 cm
Week 4: 4.4 cm   Week 8: ?

1. What type of graph will you use to display your data? Why?

   _____

2. Draw your graph and be sure to write a title and label the x and y axes.

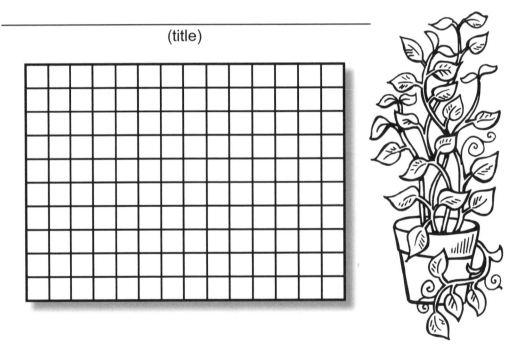

_____
(title)

3. Explain how you decided on the increments for your graph.

   _____

   _____

4. Predict the height of the plant in Week 8. Explain your prediction.

   _____

   _____

Name _____

Summer Fun

How do you like to spend your summer vacation?

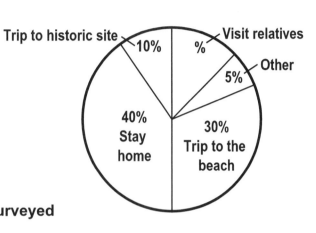

Summer Vacation

Trip to historic site — 10%
Visit relatives
%
Other
5%
40% Stay home
30% Trip to the beach

200 people surveyed

1. Use the circle graph to answer these questions. Be sure to explain your answers.

    a) What percentage likes to visit relatives?

    _____

    b) How many people like to visit relatives?

    _____

2. Write three questions that can be answered with the data on the graph. Answer each question.

    _____

    _____

    _____

    _____

3. Write two conclusions you can draw from this data.

    _____

    _____

4. Who might be interested in this information? Why?

    _____

    _____

Name _____

On a Roll

It's time to make some predictions!

1. When rolling two dice and adding the numbers rolled, which sum are you most likely to get? Justify your prediction.

   _____

2. Which sum are you least likely to get? Justify your prediction.

   _____

3. Now test your predictions. Roll two dice 40 times and record the sums on the line plot below. Be sure to include a title.

   _____

   (title)

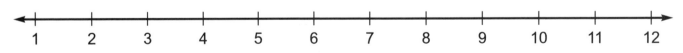

4. Did your data match your predictions? Explain your answer.

   _____
   _____
   _____
   _____
   _____

Reproducible

Name _____

What Are the Chances?

You have a bag with 5 blue marbles, 3 green marbles, 8 yellow marbles, and 4 red marbles.

1. If you pick one marble out of the bag without looking, what is the probability that it will be yellow? Explain your answer.

   _____

2. What is the probability that the marble you pick will be blue? Explain your answer.

   _____

3. What is the probability that the marble you pick will be green or blue? Explain your answer.

   _____

   _____

4. If you pick a marble 100 times, replacing the marble after each pick, about how many times would you expect to pick a blue? Explain your answer.

   _____

   _____

5. What is the difference between experimental probability and theoretical probability? Use the probability example above to help explain each term.

   _____

   _____

   _____

   _____

6. Would you be more confident about an experimental probability based on 20 trials or 100 trials (picks from the marble bag)? Why?

   _____

   _____

   _____

   _____

   _____

© Good Apple GA13072   Reproducible   **59**

Name _____

flipping over Probability

Heads or tails? What's the probability?

1. If you flipped a coin four times, what are all possible outcomes? List these below.

2. What is the theoretical probability that you will get four tails? Explain your answer.

   _____

   _____

3. What is the theoretical probability that you will get one head and three tails? Explain your answer.

   _____

   _____

4. What is the theoretical probability that you will get two heads and two tails? Explain your answer.

   _____

   _____

5. If you flip a coin four times, will the theoretical probability of getting two heads and two tails always be the same? Justify your answer.

   _____

   _____

6. If you flip a coin four times, will the experimental probability of getting two heads and two tails always be the same? Justify your answer.

   _____

   _____

Reproducible

Name _____

Help at Hangman

You are playing Hangman and want some information to help you choose the most frequently used letters. You would like to know which vowels appear most often in words. Set up and conduct an experiment to determine which vowel has the greatest probability of being used in a word. Explain your experiment and describe the results.

_____
_____
_____
_____
_____
_____
_____
_____
_____
_____
_____
_____
_____
_____
_____
_____
_____
_____
_____
_____
_____
_____
_____

Name _____

Cupcakes for Sale

Your class has planned a cupcake fund-raiser. The supplies you have purchased are listed below. Your goal is to sell 120 cupcakes for 25 cents each.

1. Figure out your expenses and determine your profits for the cupcake sale. Explain how you figured out both expenses and profit.

Materials for signs and flyers	$4.50
Napkins	3 packs of 50 at $2.50/pack
Cupcakes (made by a local bakery)	$1.50/dozen

   _____

   _____

   _____

   _____

2. How might you change the fund-raiser so that it will yield a greater profit?

   _____

   _____

   _____

3. Design another class fund-raiser. Explain your expenses and profits.

   _____

   _____

   _____

   _____

   _____

   _____

Reproducible

Name _____

Calling All Students

The seventh grade had a phone tree so that all students could be called and reminded to bring cookies for the carnival bake sale. One student was asked to begin by phoning three students. Each of those students phoned three more students. Then each of those students phoned three other students. Each student received only one phone call, and all of the seventh graders were phoned.

1. How many students were in the seventh grade? Use the space below to solve the problem; then explain your answer.

_____

_____

_____

2. Each student brought a dozen cookies for the bake sale. The cookies were sold at a price of three cookies for $1.00. How much money was made from the sale? Use the space below to solve the problem; then explain your answer.

_____

_____

_____

Number Stumpers

Here are some clever number questions to challenge you!

1. The sum of two numbers is 11. The product of the same numbers is 18. What are the two numbers? _____, _____

2. The sum of two numbers is 12. The product of the same numbers is 35. What are the two numbers? _____, _____

3. The sum of two numbers is 16. The product of the same numbers is 63. What are the two numbers? _____, _____

4. Explain the strategy you used to solve these problems.

   _____

   _____

   _____

5. Make each of these equations true by filling the spaces with a sign (+, –, x, ÷). Remember the order of operations.

   a) $5 \times 6 \_\_\_ 2 - 7 = 53$ c) $3 \times 8 \_\_\_ 6 - 8 = -4$

   b) $6 + 12 \_\_\_ 3 - 2 = 8$ d) $7 + 4 \_\_\_ 6 + 8 = 39$

6. Explain the strategy you used to find the missing operation signs.

   _____

   _____

   _____

   _____

   _____

Name _____

Decisions! Decisions!

Congratulations! You're going to select a new bike at the bike shop!

1. You can choose from 5-speed or 10-speed bikes. Your bike can be silver, black, red, or gold. You can get a bike that has a headlight or one with no light. How many different bike combinations do you have to choose from? List the choices below.

2. Explain the strategy you used to solve this problem.

    _____

    _____

3. If you could also choose a black seat or a red seat, how many bicycle choices would you have? Use the space below to solve the problem and then explain how you got your answer.

    _____

    _____

4. Which bike would you choose?

    _____

Name _____

field Trip finances

1. Mrs. Corker's class was going on a field trip to see a science film at the theater. Complete the table below to show the cost of admission for 1–8 students.

# of students	1	2	3	4	5	6	7	8
Total cost	$3.25	$6.50						

2. Think about what is happening in the table. Write an equation to show the relationship between the total admission cost a and the number of students s. _____

3. Use your equation to find the cost of admission for

   a) 18 students _____

   b) 72 students _____

4. Is there any benefit in using an equation rather than a table to solve these problems? Explain.

   _____

   _____

5. If the teacher paid $87.75, how many students were admitted to the theater? Explain how you figured out your answer.

   _____

   _____

6. The bus cost for the trip was $83.00. If the total cost (bus and admission) was $157.75, how many students were admitted to the theater? Explain how you determined the answer.

   _____

   _____

   _____

Name _____

An Amusing Trip

Don't let these number stories "trip" you up!

1. Julio went to the amusement park. He spent $\frac{1}{2}$ of his money on admission, and $\frac{1}{2}$ of what he had left on refreshments. Julio also spent $2.75 on a balloon. When he left the park, Julio had $6.45. How much did he have to start? Use the space below to solve the problem and then explain your answer.

_____

_____

_____

2. Kate also went to the amusement park. She bought tickets for the carnival games, but only used $\frac{1}{4}$ of them. Kevin took $\frac{1}{2}$ of what Kate had left, then Joe took $\frac{1}{3}$ of what was left. Finally, Rita took the last two tickets from Kate. How many tickets did Kate buy in the first place? Use the space below to solve the problem and then explain your answer.

_____

_____

_____

_____

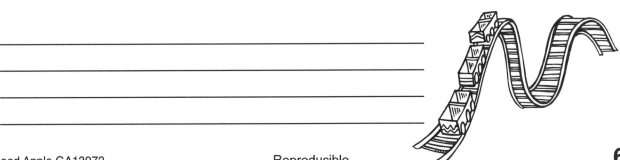

Name _____

What's the Scoop?

Do you like ice cream? What's your favorite flavor? How many scoops do you like?

1. Erica had a two-scoop ice cream cone. Her cone had one scoop of vanilla and one scoop of chocolate. How many arrangements of flavors could there be for her two-scoop cone? List the arrangements below.

2. What if Erica had a three-scoop cone with one scoop of chocolate, one scoop of vanilla, and one scoop of mint chocolate chip? How many arrangements might there be for her three-scoop cone? List the arrangements below.

3. Now, what if Erica had a four-scoop cone with one scoop of each of the following flavors: chocolate, vanilla, mint chocolate chip, and butter pecan. How many different arrangements of flavors could there be for her four-scoop cone? List the arrangements below.

4. Can you find a pattern that will let you predict the number of arrangements for a ten-scoop cone with ten different flavors of ice cream? Record your data for two-scoop, three-scoop, and four-scoop cones on the table below. Complete this chart and then explain how you can figure out the number of arrangements for a ten-scoop cone without making a list of all the possible arrangements.

Number of Scoops	Number of Arrangements
1	1
2	
3	
4	
5	
6	
7	
8	
9	
10	

_____

_____

_____

Reproducible

Name _____

Think about It (1)

1. Write a summary of what you learned in today's math class.

_____

_____

_____

_____

_____

_____

_____

_____

_____

_____

_____

_____

_____

2. How will you be able to use the information you learned today? Explain your answer.

_____

_____

_____

_____

_____

_____

_____

_____

_____

_____

_____

_____

Name _____

Think about It (2)

1. What was easy about today's math lesson? What was hard?

_____

_____

_____

_____

_____

_____

_____

_____

_____

_____

_____

2. What questions do you have about today's lesson?

_____

_____

_____

_____

_____

_____

_____

_____

_____

_____

Reproducible

Name _____

Math and Other Subjects

How will knowing math help you in other subjects, such as science and social studies? Explain your answer.

_____

_____

_____

_____

_____

_____

_____

_____

_____

_____

_____

_____

_____

_____

_____

_____

_____

_____

_____

_____

Name _____

Prove Your Point

Your friend does not consider math important in his or her life. Write your friend a letter to persuade him or her that math is used every day. Include specific examples to prove your point.

_____

_____

_____

_____

_____

_____

_____

_____

_____

_____

_____

_____

_____

_____

_____

_____

_____

_____

_____

_____

_____

_____

_____

_____

Reproducible

Math on the Job

Select a career that interests you and research how math is used in that career. Write a report to describe the role of math in your possible career.

_____

_____

_____

_____

_____

_____

_____

_____

_____

_____

_____

_____

_____

_____

_____

_____

_____

_____

_____

_____

_____

_____

Answer Key

Note: Explanations and examples for open-ended items will vary. The answers supplied are guidelines, highlighting key points. To conserve space, we have not repeated *Answers will vary* for these responses.

NUMERATION

Perplexing Patterns, page 8
1. 243, 729, 2,187. Multiply by 3 or triple numbers.
2. a) 42, 35, 28. Subtract 7; descending multiples of 7.
   b) 48, 96, 192. Double numbers or multiply by 2.
   c) 40, 48, 56. Multiples of 8.
   d) 24, 30, 37. Add 2, add 3, add 4, . . .
3. 8, 7, 10, 9, 12, 11. Subtract 1, add 3 (repeat).
4. a) O, R, U. Skip two letters each time.
   b) K, P, V. Skip 0 letters, 1 letter, 2 letters, . . .

Exponent Power, page 9
1. A raised number that tells how many times the base number is being multiplied by itself.
2. Answers should say Ex-Man did this:
   $4^3 = 4 \times 4 \times 4 = 64$
3. a) 625; b) 343; c) 81; d) 216; e) 4,096;
   f) 20,736 or 1; g) 1,000,000; h) 5,153,632 or 33,554,432
4. Yes, $6^1 = 6$. Answers might say that exponents represent the number of times that the base is used as a factor.

Prime Time, page 10
1. Prime: A whole number greater than 1 with only two whole positive factors—1 and itself.
   Composite: A whole number greater than 1 that is not a prime.
2. Primes: 2, 3, 5, 7, 11, 13, 17, 19, 23
   Odds: 1, 3, 5, 7, 9, 11, 13, 15, 17, 19, 21, 23, 25
   Prime and odd: 3, 5, 7, 11, 13, 17, 19
   Answers should say that numbers appear on both lists.
3. 2. Another even number would have 2 as a factor.
4. Answer should list prime factors from smallest to largest, use exponents to group like numbers, express number as product of two primes ($3^2 \times 5$).
5. a) $2^3 \times 3$; b) 3×5; c) $2^4 \times 7$; d) $2^2 \times 3 \times 5^2$; e) $2^2 \times 19$; f) $2 \times 3 \times 5^2$

What Are LCM's?, page 11
1. LCM is the smallest number other than 0 that is a multiple of two or more numbers.
2. Find the LCM by listing multiples of each number, finding the smallest number that appears in both lists.
3. a) 36; b) 39; c) 14; d) 80; e) 100; f) 397
4. No. Answers should include that there is an infinite number of multiples.

A Number Challenge, page 12
1. 15 numbers: 6, 7, 8, 67, 68, 76, 78, 86, 87, 678, 687, 768, 786, 867, 876
2. Numbers from smallest to largest: 6, 7, 8, 67, 68, 76, 78, 86, 87, 678, 687, 768, 786, 867, 876
3. Answers should include an organized process to be sure that all possibilities have been found.

The Hidden Square, page 13
1. a) 25; b) 100; c) 169; d) 225; e) 625
2. a) 7; b) 9; c) 11; d) 16; e) 20

62	10	73	15	27	713	4	57
306	0	218	42	99	421	43	519
29	89	437	75	130	920	2	14
82	18	100	60	108	25	701	95
535	126	7	19	416	20	76	500
107	639	169	11	16	225	93	164
501	1	397	900	41	9	274	450
47	15	49	480	5	625	17	12
920	82	724	13	21	342	31	627
3	74	160	6	111	821	943	8

3. 4. Multiply 4 by itself and get 16.
4. To multiply a number by itself or raise it to the power of 2.

WHOLE NUMBERS

Why Estimate?, page 14
1. Answers may include estimating time, distances, purchases, budgets.
2. Answers will vary.

Tell Me a Story, page 15

1. $c + 5 = 8$, $c = 3$
2. $5m = 25$, $m = 5$
3. $\frac{24}{b} = 4$, $b = 6$
4. Answers should match equation. $x = 5$
5. Answers should match equation. $d = 9$
6. Answers may say to try different values for d (guess, check, revise) or to use inverse operations.

Make It Simpler, page 16

1.
$$s + 9 = 27$$
$$s + 9 - 9 = 27 - 9$$
$$s = 18$$

2.
$$15 + p = 32$$
$$15 - 15 + p = 32 - 15$$
$$p = 17$$

3.
$$10x = 120$$
$$\frac{10x}{10} = \frac{120}{10}$$
$$x = 12$$

4. No; insufficient information. Need to know the total number of people.
5. Answers should mention that deciding which operation describes what is happening, and which number facts are known or missing.

My Dear Aunt Sally, page 17

1. a) Solve within grouping symbols
   b) Simplify exponents
   c) Multiply and divide from left to right
   d) Add and subtract from left to right.
2.–4. Answers should show use of order of operations.
2. 25. Multiply, add.
3. 210. Solve parenthesis, multiply.
4. a) 112. Simplify exponent, multiply.
   b) 60. Solve parenthesis, multiply.
   c) 500. Simplify exponent, multiply.
   d) 22. Divide, subtract.
   e) 12. Solve parenthesis, multiply.
   f) 36. Multiply, add.

RATIONAL NUMBERS

Predicting Fractions, Page 18

1. $\frac{1}{5}, \frac{1}{6}, \frac{1}{7}$; denominators increase by 1.
2. a) $\frac{1}{32}, \frac{1}{64}, \frac{1}{128}$; fractions multiplied by $\frac{1}{2}$ or divided by 2.
   b) $\frac{1}{162}, \frac{1}{486}, \frac{1}{1,458}$; fractions multiplied by $\frac{1}{3}$ or divided by 3.
3. Answers will vary.

Making the Grade, page 19

1.–3. Answers should mention converting to equivalent fractions with denominators of 100.
1. 85% correct.
2. 64% received an A.
3. a) Failed, scored 50%.
   b) Passed, scored 70%.
   c) Passed, scored 80%.
   d) Passed, scored about 77%.

An Appetizing Order, page 20

1. $1.23. Answers should say how to multiply cost of each item by 9% or 0.09, round to the nearest cent.
2. Forms must list items, quantity, price each, subtotals, and shipping costs, adding up to no more than $100.
3. 6 Candy Mixes for $89.60. Answers should mention that more Mixes can be bought, since they are the cheapest item.

What's the Difference?, page 21

1. Answers may say that 5 tens = 50; 5 tenths is part or half of one whole divided into ten parts.
2. Answers may say that 12 hundreds = 1,200; 12 hundredths = 12 parts of one whole divided into 100 parts.

What's the Connection?, page 22

1. a) 0.24; b) $\frac{24}{100} = \frac{6}{25}$; c) 24%
2. Answers may mention that both represent part of a whole but are written in different ways.
3. Answers may mention that both are based on 100 but are written in different ways.

The Parking Lot Predicament, page 23

1. $\frac{1}{10}$ motorcycles, $\frac{1}{5}$ trucks, $\frac{1}{2}$ cars, $\frac{1}{5}$ bicycles
2. 0.1 motorcycles, 0.2 trucks, 0.5 cars, 0.2 bicycles
3. 10% motorcycles, 20% trucks, 50% cars, 20% bicycles
4. Check graphs.

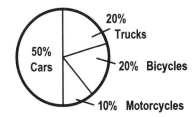

5. Answers will vary.

Can You Help?, page 24

1.–2. Answers should follow a logical sequence, comparing denominators, changing to equivalent fractions.

1. $\frac{17}{28}$

2. $\frac{11}{15}$

Palatable Portions, page 25

1. a) $\frac{1}{24}$ cup butter; b) $\frac{7}{32}$ cup sugar; c) $\frac{1}{4}$ cup flour;

   d) $\frac{1}{16}$ cup cocoa; e) $\frac{1}{4}$ teaspoon baking powder;

   f) $\frac{1}{16}$ teaspoon baking soda; g) $\frac{3}{8}$ egg;

   h) $\frac{3}{16}$ cup milk; i) $\frac{1}{8}$ teaspoon vanilla

2. Divide by 8 or multiply by $\frac{1}{8}$.

3. Yes. Answers should mention the difficulty of measuring small amounts.

4. 14 servings. Answers should say that each whole cake has 8 servings, plus 6 servings from $\frac{3}{4}$ cake.

On the Ratio Trail, page 26

1. A comparison of two quantities (e.g., 1:2, 1 to 2). Examples must compare two quantities.

2. 24:16, 6:4, or 3:2

3. a) 32:30 or 16:15; b) 16:32 or 1:2; c) 24:30 or 4:5

4. Ratios must compare two quantities from Trail Mix.

Proportional Puzzlers, page 27

1. No. Numerators and denominators must be multiplied by the same number ($\frac{2}{3} = \frac{4}{6}$).

2. A proportion is an equation stating that two ratios are equal or proportional.

3. Answers must be proportional.

4. $\frac{6}{30}$ or $\frac{1}{5}$

5. $\frac{6}{36}$ or $\frac{1}{6}$

6. 16 = x. Answers should use cross multiplication.

Delicious Deals, page 28

1. Toasty Oats 11 cents/oz.; Corn Munchies 14 cents/oz.; Checkers 12 cents/oz.; Toasty Oats is the best buy. Answers should include dividing the total cost for each cereal by the ounces in the box.

2. $9.70. Answers should multiply the weight of steak by the sale price.

3. About $5.28. Answers may include finding the difference in the price of steak on sale and at its regular price.

4. Probably an estimate. Answers should say it's hard to find a selection of potatoes weighing exactly five pounds.

A Super Sale, page 29

1. $28. Answers may say that the discount is 20%, so you are paying 80% of the original cost (.80 x 35).

2. $25.20. Answers should say that 10% off the sale price means subtracting $2.80 from the sale price.

3.

Items	Original price	Sale price 20% off	Super Saturday price Additional 10% off sale price
Video games	$ 35.00	$ 28.00	$ 25.20
CDs	$ 20.00	$ 16.00	$ 14.40
CD storage case	$ 13.00	$ 10.40	$ 9.36
Cassette tapes	$ 9.50	$ 7.60	$ 6.84
Video play station	$140.00	$112.00	$100.80

4. Answers should include the original total of all items ($217.50), total Super Saturday cost ($156.60), total savings ($60.90).

Batter Up!, page 30

1. Ryan 0.215, Kevin 0.253, Joe 0.257, Patrick 0.275, Michael 0.278, Andrew 0.279, Chris 0.290, Jason 0.301, Steven 0.310, Rodney 0.331

2. Answers should include ways to order tenths, hundredths, then thousandths.

3. Answers may include measurement, money, temperature, mileage, interest rates.

INTEGERS

Inquiring About Integers, page 31

1. Integers are whole numbers and their opposites. Zero is a whole number, so it is also an integer.

2. No. 3.5 is not a whole number, so it's not an integer.

3. Answers may include the rule that adding a negative number really means subtracting the number.

4. Answers might begin with finding the number on the line. If adding a positive number, move that many spaces to the right; if adding a negative number, move that many spaces to the left.

Positive or Negative?, page 32

1. Negative. Answers may say that you begin on the negative side and move further to the left.

2. Yes. Answers may solve each equation to show that the sums are equal or plot them on a number line.

3. Greater. Answers may say that subtracting a negative number means adding the positive of the number.

Absolutely Positive!, page 33

1. A number's distance from zero.

2. Lines should mark two opposite numbers; show they are the same distance from 0.

3. The number itself. Answers should show that the absolute value is the distance from 0 and always the number itself.

4. The number's positive opposite. Answers should show that absolute value is always opposite the positive number; distance is measured in positive units.

5. a) 3; b) 10; c) 0; d) 6.34; e) 3.5; f) $\frac{1}{2}$

Check It Out!, page 34

1. $52.00. Answers should include all amounts withdrawn, deposited, and the balance.

2.

Transaction Description	Amount of Payment or Withdrawal	Amount of Deposit	Balance
Deposit		$100.00	$100.00
Expr. Clothing	$ 32.00		$ 68.00
CD World	$ 12.00		$ 56.00
Deposit		$ 23.00	$ 79.00
Ticket Max	$ 27.00		$ 52.00

GEOMETRY

Meet Mr. or Ms. Write Angle, page 35

1. Answers should include using a protractor; reading smaller number for acute, larger for obtuse.
2. $\angle ABC = 60°$
3. Acute: 0°–90°; right: 90°; obtuse: 90°–180°
4. Answers should accurately show angles.

What's the Angle?, page 36

1. Sum of their measures equals 90°.
2. Sum of their measures equals 180°.
3. No. Sum would be greater than 180°.
4. 90°. Sum of measures of supplementary angles is 180°; other angle must also measure 90°.
5. No. Sum of two complementary angles is 90°; obtuse angle measures greater than 90°.

Do You Know Your Shapes?, page 37

1. Answers will vary, but must match definitions (2).
2. Rhombus: all sides the same length, opposite ones parallel.
Parallelogram: opposite sides the same length and parallel.
Trapezoid: exactly two sides are parallel.
3. a) True. All parallelograms have four sides.
b) False. Rhombus has opposite sides parallel.
c) False. Trapezoid may not have all sides same length; has only two sides parallel.

What Shape Is That Number?, page 38

1. 21 dots
2. 78 dots
3. Answers should include making a table or discovering a pattern.
4. 36 dots
5. 144 dots
6. Answers should include making a table or discovering a pattern (e.g., 5th square = 5^2; 11th square = 11^2).

MEASUREMENT

Metric Choices, page 39

1. cm or dm. Answers should include that most desks are less than one square meter, so meters are too large.
2. km. Answers should include that it's impractical to use smaller measures for long distances.
3. mm. Answers should include that other measures are too large to give accurate measures.
4. Answers should accurately list items in each column to correspond with chosen measures.

Going in Circles, page 40

1. Answers should include measuring distances around a figure—P around rectangles, C circles.
2. Answers should say pi is about 3.14; used to find C or A of circles.
3. Answers should include finding r or d; using pi to calculate C ($C = 2\pi r$, $C = \pi d$).
4. a) 37.68 cm; b) 18.84 inches; c) 31.4 mm

Calculating Cookies, page 41

1. Rectangular cookie. Answers should include finding areas of cookies and price/sq. inch.
10" x 14": A = 140 sq. inches; approx. 0.05 cents per sq. inch.
10" round: A = 78.5 sq. inches; approx. 0.06 cents per sq. inch.
2. Answers should relate to $A = \pi r^2$.
3. Answers should relate to $A = l \times w$.

Puzzling Parallelograms, page 42

1. Base and height measurements should be correctly labeled, dotted line drawn to indicate where height is measured.

2. $A = b \times h$; A = 5 cm x 3 cm = 15 cm^2
3. a) 72 mm^2; b) 273 m^2; c) 323 cm^2; d) 10.44 m^2; e) 598,950 km^2

Getting Ready for the Big Test, page 43

Drawings and tips will vary. Formulas:
rectangles: $A = l \times w$; squares: A = length of a side squared
parallelograms: $A = b \times h$; triangles: $A = \frac{1}{2}b \times h$
circles: $A = \pi r^2$

Sport Sketches, page 44

1. Fields should be accurately drawn to chosen scales; include title and scale.
2. Scales will vary, but entire drawing must fit in space allowed (e.g., $\frac{1}{4}$ in. = 10 yds).
3. a) 5,000 sq. yds; b) 300 yds
4. Courts should be accurately drawn to chosen scale; include title and scale.
5. Scales will vary, but entire drawing must fit in space allowed (e.g., 1 in. = 12 ft).
6. a) 2,808 sq. ft b) 228 ft

Metric Fun and Games, page 46

Answers should include rules, describe how a winner is determined, and help players understand metric measures.

STATISTICS/DATA ANALYSIS

A Matter of Age, page 47

1.
Stems	Leaves
2	1, 2, 2, 4, 4, 4, 4, 6, 8, 8, 9
3	2, 5
4	1, 1, 3, 4, 7, 9
5	
6	0

2. 39. Subtract the smallest number from largest.
3. 24. The piece of data that appears most frequently.
4. 28.5. The middle number when data has been placed in order. (Need to average the middle two numbers.)
5. 33.2. Average the data. Answers should include that the mean is greater than the median because of the outlier (60) that is averaged in with the others. The outlier has no effect on the median.
6. Answers may include comments about the mode, median, range, mean; ages of teachers in the study.

Which Would You Choose?, page 48

1. Answers may indicate a line graph to indicate trends over time.
2. Answers may indicate a bar graph or pictograph to show distinct categories of data; a circle graph to look at the whole class, determine portions that prefer different destinations.
3. Answers may indicate a stem and leaf plot to organize a lot of two-digit data so that it can be seen and interpreted easily.
4. Answers may indicate a double bar graph to compare data by grade levels.
5. Answers may indicate a line graph to indicate trends over time.

Michael's Awesome Achievements, page 49

1.
Season	Games Played	Total Points	Average Points per Game (to nearest tenth)	Scoring Rank (#1 is best)
1984–85	82	2,313	28.2	11
1985–86	18	408	22.7	13
1986–87	82	3,041	37.1	1
1987–88	82	2,868	35.0	2
1988–89	81	2,633	32.5	5
1989–90	82	2,753	33.6	3
1990–91	82	2,580	31.5	6
1991–92	80	2,404	30.1	8
1992–93	78	2,541	32.6	4
1993–94	Did not play this year.			
1994–95	17	457	26.9	12
1995–96	82	2,491	30.4	7
1996–97	82	2,431	29.6	9
1997–98	82	2,357	28.7	10
Career Totals	930	29,277	31.5	XXXX

2. Answers should include dividing the total points for the season by the total games played.
3. See the completed table. Answers should include ordering decimals from highest to lowest.
4. 31.5 points per game; 1986–87, 1987–88, 1988–89, 1989–90, 1992–93. Answers should include comparing 31.5 to other averages.

Picturing Michael's Accomplishments, page 50

1. Graphs must show Michael's average points scored per game for each season.
2. Answers may say that a line graph is a good choice as it shows data over time.
3. Answers may include trends in the data, best or worst years, consistency, decline.

The Name Game, page 51

1.

2. a) 7; b) 5; c) 5.25; d) 5
3. Yes. Answers should say that a line plot shows data well as there is a limited amount of data, a small range.
4. Answers should use math data (e.g., mean) to justify decisions.

Got the Munchies?, page 52

1. Graphs will vary but should be accurate.
2. Increments should be reasonable considering the range of data (e.g., 5, not 20).
3. Answers may mention times when people buy or don't buy candy.
4. Answers may include vending machine companies, administrators, dentists.

Top It Off! (1), page 53

1. Charts may vary, but should show the favorite toppings for ten people.
2. Predictions should be consistent with results.

Top It Off! (2), page 54

1. Answers should accurately list group results.

2. Answers should include title, labels, reasonable increments, accurate data.

Top It Off! (3), page 55

1. Answers should include fractions or percents to describe the most popular toppings for children and adults.

2.–4. Answers should be based on data collected.

Watching It Grow, page 56

1. Answers may say that line graphs display data over time.

2. Graphs should include title, labels, reasonable increments, accurate data.

3. Answers should be reasonable considering the range.

4. Predictions should be consistent with the trends.

Summer Fun, page 57

1. a) 15%. Answers should include adding percents, subtracting the sum from 100%.

   b) 30 people. Answers should include that 15% of 200 people visited relatives.

2. Questions and answers should be accurately based on the graph.

3. Answers should be accurately based on the graph.

4. Answers should be related to graph information.

PROBABILITY

On a Roll, page 58

1. Answers may say 7 because there are six ways to get 7 (6 + 1, 5 + 2, 4 + 3, 3 + 4, 2 + 5, 1 + 6).

2. Answers may say that you are least likely to get 2 (1 + 1) or 12 (6 + 6). Rolling a sum of 1 is impossible.

3. Answers will vary.

4. Answers will vary.

What Are the Chances?, page 59

1. $\frac{8}{20}$ or $\frac{2}{5}$. Answers should indicate that 8 out of 20 marbles are yellow.

2. $\frac{5}{20}$ or $\frac{1}{4}$. Answers should indicate that 5 out of 20 marbles are blue.

3. $\frac{8}{20}$ or $\frac{2}{5}$. Answers should indicate that there are 3 green and 8 blue, making 8 green or blue marbles out of 20.

4. 25 out of 100. Answers may say the probability of picking blue is $\frac{5}{20}$ or $\frac{1}{4}$, regardless the number of picks.

5. Experimental probability is what actually happens in an experiment. Theoretical probability is the ratio of the number of ways that an event can happen to the total number of possible outcomes. Examples should use data accurately.

6. 100 trials. Experimental probability becomes closer to theoretical probability as the number of trials increases.

Flipping over Probability, page 60

1. HHHH   THHT
   HHHT   HTHT
   HHTH   THTH
   HTHH   TTTH
   THHH   TTHT
   HHTT   THTT
   HTTH   HTTT
   TTHH   TTTT

2. $\frac{1}{16}$. Answers should say that four tails appears once out of 16 possible outcomes.

3. $\frac{4}{16}$. Answers should say that one head, three tails appears four times out of 16.

4. $\frac{6}{16}$, or $\frac{3}{8}$. Answers should say that two heads, two tails appears six times out of 16.

5. Theoretical probability remains the same because it's based on possible outcomes.

6. Experimental probability may vary, as actual outcomes are uncertain.

Help at Hangman, page 61

Answers should explain the experiment and describe results.

PROBLEM SOLVING

Cupcakes for Sale, page 62

1. Expenses: $27.00. Add costs for signs and flyers, napkins, cakes. Profit: $3.00. Sale made $30.00 but $27.00 was used to pay expenses.

2. Answers should include a plan to increase profits by raising the price of cakes, selling more, decreasing expenses in some way.

3. Answers will vary.

Calling All Students, page 63

1. 40 students. Answers should include drawing a diagram.

2. $160.00. 40 students x 12 cookies each = 480 cookies. Cookies sold for 3/$1.00; 480 ÷ 3 = $160.00.

Number Stumpers, page 64

1. 9, 2
2. 7, 5
3. 9, 7
4. Answers may include guess, check, revise.
5. a) x; b) ÷; c) ÷; d) x
6. Answers may include guess, check, revise.

Decisions! Decisions!, page 65

1. 16: 5/silver with/without light, 5/black with/without light, 5/red with/without light, 5/gold with/without light, 10/silver with/without light, 10/black with/without light, 10/red with/without light, 10/gold with/without light.
2. Answers should include an organized list or diagram.
3. 32. Answers should include adding new options to the list or diagram.

Field Trip Finances, page 66

1.

Students	1	2	3	4	5	6	7	8
Cost	$3.25	$6.50	$9.75	$13.00	$16.25	$19.50	$22.75	$26.00

2. $a = 3.25s$
3. a) $a = 3.25 \times 18$. Cost for 18 = $58.50.
   b) $a = 3.25 \times 72$. Cost for 72 = $234.00.
4. Answers should mention that large numbers need large tables, so equations are helpful.
5. 27 students. Answers should use the equation (2).
6. 23 students. Answers should include subtracting the cost of the bus from the total cost to find the cost of admission; dividing the admission by the cost/student.

An Amusing Trip, page 67

1. $36.80. Answers should involve working backwards.
2. 8 tickets. Answers may involve working backwards or using guess and check.

What's the Scoop?, page 68

1. 2: c, v (chocolate, vanilla), v, c (vanilla, chocolate)
2. 6: c, v, m; c, m, v; v, c, m; v, m, c; m, c, v; m, v, c
3. 24: v, c, m, b; v, c, b, m; v, m, b, c; v, m, c, b; v, b, m, c; v, b, c, m; c, v, m, b; c, v, b, m; c, m, b, v; c, m, v, b; c, b, m, v; c, b, v, m; m, c, v, b; m, c, b, v; m, v, c, b; m, v, b, c; m, b, c, v; m, b, v, c; b, v, c, m; b, v, m, c; b, c, v, m; b, c, m, v; b, m, c, v; b, m, v, c.
4. Answers may include multiplying the number of scoops by the number of arrangements from the preceding row of the table (e.g., 10 = 10 x arrangements for 9 scoops); or multiply 1 x 2 x 3 x 4 x 5 x 6 x 7 x 8 x 9 x 10.

Number of Scoops	Number of Arrangements
1	1
2	2
3	6
4	24
5	120
6	720
7	5,040
8	40,320
9	362,880
10	3,628,800

REFLECTIONS, pages 69–73

Answers will vary for all questions.